A Southern Woman's Guide to Herbs

A SOUTHERN WOMAN'S GUIDE TO HERBS

⊷⊷❈⊹⊹⊷

JACLYN WELDON WHITE

MERCER UNIVERSITY PRESS | MACON, GEORGIA

MUP/P472

First Edition

Book design by Burt&Burt

Photography by Jaclyn Weldon White unless otherwise credited
Photo of teas on page 29 by Mary-Frances Burt
Photos on pages 12 and 26 by Bigstock
Photo on page 49 by FoodPhotoSite.com

Books published by Mercer University Press are printed on acid-free
paper that meets the requirements of the American National Standard for
Information Sciences—Permanence of Paper for Printed Library Materials.

Mercer University Press is a member of Green Press Initiative (greenpressinitiative.org),
a nonprofit organization working to help publishers and printers increase their use of recycled paper
and decrease their use of fiber derived from endangered forests.
This book is printed on recycled paper.

ISBN 978-0-88146-460-3

Library of Congress Cataloging-in-Publication Data

White, Jaclyn Weldon.
A Southern woman's guide to herbs / Jaclyn Weldon White.
pages cm
Includes index.
ISBN 978-0-88146-460-3 (pbk. : alk. paper) — ISBN 0-88146-460-0 (pbk. : alk. paper)
1. Cooking (Herbs) 2. Sedge craft. 3. Herb gardening—Southern States. I. Title.
TX819.H4W46 2013
641.6'57—dc23

2013027494

To Shannon, my beloved daughter,
who has taught me the true meaning of strength.

Introduction

ARDENING NEVER INTERESTED ME WHEN I WAS GROWING UP, but my sweet mother could hardly leave a spot of soil untouched. Our suburban yard was always awash in blooms. One summer when the gardenia bushes were in full flower, we were scheduled to leave town for a week's vacation. Mother couldn't bear leaving those wonderful blossoms behind. She picked nearly every one, packed them in wet paper towels and plastic wrap and layered them in two cardboard suit boxes. When we arrived at our rented Florida beach house, she unpacked the gardenias. For the week we were there, every room was filled with bowls of flowers and intoxicating fragrance.

While my mother had an almost magical touch with plants and a love of all things botanical, it didn't rub off on her eldest child. I enjoyed the flowers as anyone enjoys a pleasant background, but I never had a desire to put my hands in the dirt and do anything about producing them—until I discovered herbs.

Herbs are generally defined as plants that are helpful to humankind, but definitions vary from one person to the next. Some people think of them only as those dried leaves that are added to food during cooking while others include myriad plants—from lumber-supplying hardwoods to those farm crops that produce clothing fibers—in that list. I usually consider herbs to be plants that contribute to food, medicines, crafts, and cosmetics, but you should feel free to make up your own definition. Everybody else does.

Herbs have been used for thousands of years. From before recorded history, people in Europe, Asia, Australia, Africa, and the Americas gathered herbs for food, healing, and the practice of magic. These plants were an integral part of everyday living. Some of the most exalted positions in any tribe were reserved for those elders with a knowledge of herbal craft.

Today, most people hardly give herbs a passing thought unless they are using them as culinary flavoring. We're much more familiar with the finished products (whether medicines or cosmetics) than their sources in nature.

As recently as a hundred years ago, people had much closer relationships with herbs. Physicians, apothecaries, and healers kept an arsenal of these plants on hand to treat everything from angina to insomnia, just as their ancestors had. The cures, mostly the product of trial and error, were passed down from one generation to the next and became ingrained in the fabric of the society.

References to herbs and other plants are sprinkled throughout Shakespeare's plays and sonnets. The most famous is probably a line spoken by Ophelia in Hamlet: "There's rosemary, that's for remembrance" (Act IV, sc. 5). Rosemary signified remembrance long before the bard ever wrote that line. Recent studies at North Umbria University in the United Kingdom, one in 2003 and another in 2012, indicate that rosemary enhances the overall quality of memory and may improve brain function.

The Bible contains numerous herbal mentions. Psalm 51:7 states, "Cleanse me with hyssop and I will be clean." Hyssop, a member of the mint family, was used by the Israelites in ceremonial rituals. Burning hyssop was believed to achieve inner cleansing. Mint and rue were mentioned as tithes in Luke and you'll find garlic in Numbers and mustard in Matthew. In Isaiah 35:1, we find "The desert shall rejoice and blossom; like the rose."

Roses hold a special places in antiquity. The oldest known fossils of roses date back 35 million years. The flowers were mentioned in Sumerian writings, circa 2800 BC and were considered sacred in ancient Egypt. Dried roses, formed into funeral wreaths, have been found in Egyptian tombs.

I never thought much about herbs myself. I certainly wasn't considering them twenty-something years ago when I was dabbling in genealogical research. Then I discovered my husband's great-grandfather Joseph R. White. In the late 1800s and early 1900s, he lived in Gwinnett County, Georgia. A deaf man who couldn't speak, he had quite a reputation in that rural area as a healer. I learned that he often concocted tonics and medicines from herbs. According to local legend, one time several of his neighbors became ill from a poisonous plant they'd encountered in the woods. They appealed to Joseph for help, and he brewed a potion that cured them all.

For some reason, that story fired my imagination. While I didn't aspire to become a healer myself, I was intrigued with the idea of growing my own herbs and using them to flavor food or scent the air in the house. I pictured neat garden rows of lush, sweet-smelling plants. Just the idea of it made me feel like some kind of earth mother in harmony with nature.

The reality, however, was something very different. My first attempt at an herb garden was dismal. I went to a local nursery and found some plants with familiar names. I chose a spot in the backyard, dug holes and put them in the ground. I watered them and waited for my garden to grow.

Unfortunately, I didn't know anything about preparing the soil, what conditions were most favorable for which herbs, or how to care for them. My "garden" was a sad, rocky place where plants struggled to survive. That first year I managed to harvest a few culinary herbs, but except for tossing them in salads, I really didn't know what I was doing. I had a long way to go.

I was discouraged, but not enough to quit. I was determined to master the task and kept trying. Over the next years, I buckled down to learn about growing herbs. I read books, watched my gardening friends, and asked hundreds of questions of some very understanding professionals.

The work paid off. I eventually had a beautiful, flourishing garden and supplied not only myself, but also my friends and neighbors with fresh herbs. Now, with twenty years' experience behind me, I'm confident with the process. I expect my plants to thrive, and I'm rarely disappointed. It's time to share what I've learned.

Growing the herbs is only the first step in the process. I cook with them, of course, but have also found plenty of other uses for these wonderful plants. They can be used to treat burns, repel insects, and create lovely, one-of-a-kind gifts. They provide ground cover and colorful landscapes, and they attract a variety of birds, bees, and butterflies.

Summer is the time
for bicycles, shade trees,
and growing herbs.

This caterpillar enjoying the last of the fall parsley
will be a beautiful butterfly in the spring.

CHAPTER 1

Cultivation

HERBS ARE NOT DIFFICULT TO GROW if you take the time to prepare the soil and plant them in the right locations. Most herbs need a good six hours of sun a day. While they can survive in rocky soil, herbs hate having wet feet, so good drainage is important. There are, however, some plants (such as mints) that can't tolerate that much sun and actually thrive in moist locations. A list of the most common herbs and the best locations for them can be found later in this chapter.

Once you select a place for your garden, remove any grass or other plants growing there. Ideally you should dig up the soil about a foot deep. This can be hard work, especially in our dense Georgia clay. My advice is to find someone to do it for you if you can. Husbands or strapping teenaged sons are both good choices. If you do have to go it alone, a pick ax is a good way to start. These fierce-looking tools do a great job of loosening the dirt and you'll feel quite empowered swinging one.

Especially if your soil has a heavy clay content, mixing a small amount of garden sand into the earth you've dug up will help with drainage. You can also amend it with compost or garden soil purchased at your nursery or hardware store. Finally, you may want to add a small amount of lime (from the same hardware store) to the mix since many herbs prefer soil that is more alkaline than acidic.

One piece of advice I can't stress too strongly is to find an herb farm near you and get to know the people who operate it. I go to the

A sunny, well-drained site

3

Olive Forge Herb Farm in Haddock, Georgia, just outside of Milledgeville. The proprietors, Darryl and Marsha Herren, know more about growing and using herbs than I'll ever learn. Even though their farm is a two-hour drive from my north Georgia home, I buy my plants there every year.

Any questions I've ever had—like where to plant a certain herb, the best way to harvest a plant, how to use particular herbs in cooking—they've answered. Their expertise doesn't end with plants. I have called Darryl any number of times to describe a strange insect or an unusual bird I've seen at the feeder. He listens, considers, and then tells me what he thinks I've seen. In twelve years he's never been wrong.

Some herbs are perennials, meaning they come back year after year. Some are annuals that live only one season, and there are even some that are biennials, which live for two years.

Many herbs grow well from seeds. If you choose to take that route, follow the directions on the seed packets as to depth and distance between plants. I'm much too impatient to do it this way and prefer to purchase the plants themselves. If you aren't close to an herb farm, you can usually find a good selection of potted culinary herbs at most large nurseries.

Once established in the garden, herbs need little ongoing maintenance. Keep the weeds away, of course, and water them—but only when the soil is dry. Remember, the quickest way to kill an herb is to drown it.

There are two schools of thought about fertilizer. Some growers use it in small quantities. It will produce greener, more lush plants. Other growers are purists and believe that herbs fed on fertilizer aren't as flavorful as those left to their own devices. I come down on the side of fertilizer. About once a month I use one of the spray-on kinds that attach to the garden hose. I haven't noticed any decrease in my herbs' flavor, and I love all that dense green growth through the summer.

Rosemary ready for sale at Olive Forge Herb Farm

A Southern Woman's Guide to Herbs

Herb—*Perennials*	Sun/Shade	Soil
bay	sun, afternoon shade	well-drained, moist
bergamot/bee balm	part shade	rich, light, moist
catnip	part shade	well-drained
chamomile	sun	light, well-drained
chives	sun, light shade	rich, well-drained
curry plant	sun	rich, well-drained
fennel	sun, afternoon shade	well-drained loam
horseradish	sun	light, moist
lavender	sun	sandy, alkaline
lemon balm	sun, afternoon shade	moist, well-drained
lemon verbena	sun	light, alkaline
marjoram	sun	rich, alkaline
mints	part shade	moist, well-drained
oregano	sun	rich, alkaline
rosemary	sun	very well-drained
sage	sun	light, dry, alkaline
savory	sun	light, alkaline
scented geranium	sun	well-drained, rich
tarragon (Mexican/Texan)	sun	rich, light, dry
thyme	sun	light, well-drained
yarrow	sun, light shade	moist, rich

Herb—*Annuals*		
basil	sun, afternoon shade	rich, light
chervil	sun	light, well-drained
cilantro	sun	rich, light
dill	sun	rich, well-drained

Herb—*Biennial*		
parsley	sun, light shade	rich, moist

Herbs in nice, neat gardens are certainly pretty. They can be laid out in simple, straight lines or can be quite intricate. With a little Internet research, you can find diagrams and instructions for gardens of many different designs and themes—Elizabethan knot gardens, fragrance gardens, kitchen gardens, biblical gardens, Shakespeare gardens, and more.

However you choose to lay out your garden, you don't need a large area for growing herbs. In a space as small as three by five feet, a gardener can raise enough thyme, basil, rosemary, and oregano to keep her kitchen supplied all summer long and still have plenty of herbs leftover for drying or freezing.

In fact there's no reason that herbs must be confined to dedicated gardens. They can be used in various ways in your landscape. A stand of bee balm can make a brilliant scarlet statement against a white wall

Bee balm

or fence, and you'll have the added benefit of attracting bees and hummingbirds.

Rosemary, with its late winter blooms, makes a lovely specimen plant. Scented geraniums beside your front door will greet visitors with the welcoming aroma of rose or lemon when they brush against the leaves. Hops, grapes, and many roses are vigorous climbers. Plant them along a fence or in front of a trellis and let them go. By mid summer you'll have a colorful accent.

Another popular use for herbs is ground cover. Many grow densely and discourage weed growth and they offer the extra benefit of fragrance when you walk on them. In shady areas, try sweet woodruff, violets, or ivy. Peppermint, wintergreen, spearmint, and countless other mints will thrive in moist, partly shaded areas. But beware: kudzu has nothing on mint. Most mints spread relentlessly and will try to take over your yard (and your neighbors') if not contained.

Scented geraniums beside a front door

Sun-loving herbs such as creeping thymes, some low-growing oreganos, golden marjoram, and others do well when planted between paving or stepping stones. They keep the weeds down, they're attractive, and they act like living mulch.

When the growing season is over and the first freeze has come, your herbs will begin to die back. Cut away the dried leaves and stems and cover your perennial herbs with mulch. I use pine straw, but any good mulch will do. Come the spring, uncover them, trim off any dead leaves and branches, and you'll be ready for another growing season.

In the South several herbs are available all year long. Rosemary, of course, is evergreen and if you check under your layer of mulch, even during the coldest months, you're likely to find thyme, marjoram or oregano growing happily beneath their protective winter cover. Cut what you want, just make sure to cover up the plant afterwards.

Herbs grow well in small areas.

CHAPTER 2

Preserving Your Herbs

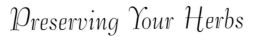

MANY FRESH HERBS FROM YOUR GARDEN are only available through the warm months. However, with a little effort, you can have them on hand all year long.

DRYING HERBS

Herbs have been preserved this way for thousands of years and I think it's still the best method. Ideally, you should harvest herbs for drying before they have flowered and the best time of day to do so is in the morning after the dew has dried away.

Wash your herbs in a sink filled with clean water. Swish them around several times to loosen dust and dirt. Lay them out on kitchen or paper towels and blot them dry. Tie the herbs in small bunches with twine and hang them in a warm, dark place with good ventilation. If you don't have a place away from daylight, you can slip a paper bag over the bunch of herbs and tie it as well. Just make sure there are holes for ventilation and that the leaves don't touch the bag.

Most herbs take one to three weeks to dry. Check them about once a week. To see if they are sufficiently dry, remove a leaf and rub it between your fingers. If it crumbles easily, it's properly dried.

When the herbs are dried, remove the leaves from the stems and store them in airtight glass jars. While you can certainly grind or chop

Herbs drying

them at this point, you'll preserve the flavor better by leaving them whole and crumbling or powdering them at the time you use them.

Another method for drying herbs is to remove the leaves from the stems and lay them in a single layer on a flat surface, such as a cookie sheet. Place them in a dark, warm, well-ventilated space. These herbs will need to be turned over every few days so that all sides are exposed to the air. They, too, will dry in one to three weeks.

There are certainly quicker ways to dry herbs. You can place them on a cookie sheet and let them dry in a 200-degree oven, turning them every 15 minutes or so. Check the herbs often. When they're crumbly, they're ready.

The microwave is another option. Place the leaves in one layer on a paper towel and cover with a second paper towel. Heat on high for 1 minute. If the herbs are not as dried as you desire, continue the process in 15-second intervals.

The oven and microwave methods are quick, but you'll lose some intensity of flavor if you dry your herbs this way.

Dried herbs ready for the pantry

Freezing Herbs

The advantage to freezing herbs is that they retain their color and you can often use them in the same way you would fresh herbs. Basils and mints are especially good candidates for freezing.

Harvest, wash and dry the herbs as described above. Remove the leaves from the stems and place them in a single layer on a plate or pan and put them in the freezer for twenty-four hours. Once frozen, they can be packed into plastic bags and stored in the freezer until you're ready to use them.

A second freezing option is to place about 1 tablespoon of whole or chopped herbs into the individual compartments of an ice tray. Top off with water and freeze. Once frozen, the cubes can be stored in plastic bags. Just thaw to use or drop a whole cube in stews or soups.

Single leaves or edible flowers frozen in ice cubes are nice in drinks. What could be prettier in a gin and tonic than pansies floating in the ice?

CHAPTER 3

Culinary Uses

NOW YOUR HERBS ARE GROWING, you're proud of your accomplishment and your neighbors are impressed with your flourishing landscape. It's summer and time to have some fun with what you're producing.

Let's start in the kitchen. I'm of the opinion that herbs improve the flavor of just about any food. They make it easy to perk up most dishes—a bay leaf or two in a pot of chili, fresh basil melted in butter to sauté a steak, or even a sprinkle of finely chopped lemon balm on fresh melon. You'll be surprised at how bright and fresh your food will taste. In no time at all, you're going to be adding herbs to everything.

PANTRY STAPLES

Here are some easy herbal additions to your pantry. With an assortment of fresh or dried herbs on hand, you can work wonders with everyday meals.

BOUQUET GARNI
3 sprigs flat-leaf parsley
2 sprigs thyme
2 sprigs marjoram
1 bay leaf

Tie all the ingredients together with butcher's twine. This classic French combination of seasonings can be dropped into simmering stews or soups. Remember to remove it before serving.

HERBAL SALT

8 tablespoons coarse kosher salt

1–2 teaspoons dried marjoram

2 teaspoons dried rosemary

2 teaspoons dried sage

Place the herbs in a blender or food processor and grind for 5 to 15 seconds. Add the salt and pulse once or twice. Pour into a bowl. You may have to remove accumulated salt from the bottom of the blender with a rubber spatula. Stir a few times in the bowl; then put the mixture in a shaker bottle. This flavored salt can be used in cooking or put right on the table. In a pretty container, it makes a nice gift.

Herbal salt

DRY HERB RUB *for Beef or Pork Roast*

2 tablespoons chopped fresh herbs—thyme, marjoram, or rosemary
    work well. (If using dried herbs, use two teaspoons.)

7 cloves of garlic, minced fine

2 tablespoons coarse kosher salt

1 1/2 teaspoons freshly ground pepper

Mix the salt, garlic and pepper together; stir in the herbs. Rub the mixture over the roast and let it stand at room temperature for one hour. Then roast as usual.

HERBED BUTTER

1 stick butter, softened

1 cup minced fresh herbs—tarragon, thyme, lemon thyme, or whatever appeals to you. (If you're using dried herbs, use only 1/4 of cup.)

Mix the two ingredients together well, then shape the butter into a log, wrap it in plastic wrap and refrigerate at least 2 hours. The butter can be used as a spread for bread or crackers. You can also put a pat of it on fish or meat during grilling. Herbed butter can be frozen for up to 2 months.

HERBAL VINEGARS

To make herbal vinegar, use any herb or combination of herbs that appeals to you. The most commonly used are basil, tarragon, rosemary, and thyme. They're all delicious, and opal basil has the added benefit of turning the vinegar a gorgeous pink color.

Bring white wine or apple cider vinegar to a boil. Remove from the heat and let it cool a minute or two. Take a generous handful of your chosen fresh herb (which you've already washed) and bruise the leaves with your hands. Put the crushed herbs into a large glass jar or bottle and pour the hot vinegar over them. Further bruise the herbs with the handle of a wooden spoon and stir the mixture a few times. Seal the container and store your vinegar in a cool, dark place for a month or two, gently shaking the bottle every week.

When the vinegar is ready, strain it (discard the herbs) and put it in a nice bottle. If

Rosemary vinegar

you like, you can put a couple of new sprigs of fresh herbs into the vinegar for decoration, but this isn't necessary. Your vinegar is now ready to use or to give as a gift.

Herbal vinegar can be used in a variety of ways. A tablespoon or two adds a nice tang to stews or soups. It makes wonderful salad dressings and can be used when grilling fish or meat.

FLAVORED HONEY

When I first heard about flavored honey, I couldn't believe how easy it was to make or what a nice impression it made when served. Several herbs, especially the sweet or floral ones, blend beautifully with honey. Rose-scented geranium will give it a delicate flowery flavor. Lemon balm and lemon verbena impart a bright citrusy touch. Thyme honey is said to be good for sore throats and honey infused with lavender is floral and tangy. It's one of my favorites, but unusual enough to be an acquired taste.

You can, of course, purchase honey in a grocery store, but I'd recommend searching out your local farmers' markets to find honey produced in your area. It's said that local honey benefits allergy sufferers because it contains traces of pollen from plants growing in the area and boosts immune systems. I don't know if that's true, but I like the idea of supporting local growers.

To make flavored honey, pour a jar of honey into a saucepan and heat it just to the point of

Rose geranium honey

boiling. Don't boil it! If you do, you'll never get rid of the resulting bubbles. Remove it from the heat. Add a generous handful or two of washed, bruised, fresh herbs and mix them into the warm honey. Then bring it once more up to a simmer. Repeat the cooling and heating process several times. The flavor will intensify each time the honey is heated.

Once it's reached the desired intensity and while it's still warm, strain the honey. Discard the herbs and pour the honey into sealable jars. Flavored honey can be used instead of sugar in cooking and it's especially good to sweeten hot teas. It's also a nice accompaniment to pancakes, waffles or, best of all, biscuits.

HERBAL SYRUP
1 cup sugar
1 cup water
handful of herbs—peppermint, lemon verbena, lemon balm, bee
  balm, and rose geranium are good choices

Heat the sugar and water in a saucepan over medium heat, stirring until the sugar is completely dissolved. Then bruise the herbs and add them to the syrup. Stir and allow the syrup to come to a boil. Remove it from the heat and let it cool a bit. Bring it to a boil again. Remove from the heat a second time and allow it to cool for 10 to 15 minutes. Then strain the syrup, discard the herbs, and pour it into a bottle.

Herbal syrup will keep for several weeks in the refrigerator. It's good poured over ice cream (even better if you heat it for several seconds in the microwave before pouring it) and can be used to sweeten tea or coffee. Diluted with club soda, it makes a refreshing iced drink.

PESTO
3 cloves of garlic
3/4 cup grated Parmesan or Romano cheese
1/4 cup pine nuts
3 packed cups of fresh basil leaves
1/2 cup olive oil
pinch of coarse kosher salt
fresh ground pepper to taste

A big reward for growing basil is that you can make your own pesto.

Put the first 3 ingredients in a food processor or blender and pulse a few times. Then add the basil and blend. Gradually drizzle in the olive oil and blend the mixture until it is smooth. Add salt and pepper to taste.

Pesto is delicious tossed with pasta, as a topping on a baked potato or on toasted bread for crostini. You can freeze leftover pesto in ice cube trays. Once frozen, remove the cubes, place them in plastic bags and store in the freezer for later use.

PARTY FOOD

Hors d'oeuvres and party snacks are terrific ways to display your new herbal expertise. Serve a few of these tasty treats at your next tea or cocktail party and be prepared to graciously (and modestly) accept the praise that follows.

CROSTINI

Now that you have pesto, the next step is to make a tasty crostini.

Toast thin slices of French bread or use bagel chips. Rub a sliced garlic clove over the top of the bread, drizzle with olive oil and spread with pesto. Serve on a pretty platter.

HERBED CREAM CHEESE

16 ounces softened cream cheese
1 tablespoon lemon juice
3 tablespoons finely chopped fresh herbs—sage, thyme, just use what you like. (If you're using dried herbs, use only one tablespoon.)
salt and pepper to taste

Mix all the ingredients well, place the mixture in a ramekin and refrigerate at least 2 hours. Serve as a spread for bread or crackers. If you mix it with a tablespoon or two of sour cream, you can also use this as a thick dip for cut raw vegetables.

SMOKED SALMON SPREAD

8 ounces softened cream cheese

1/2 cup sour cream

2 tablespoons minced green onions

1 tablespoon minced fresh herbs (dill or basil are my favorites, but try others as well)

1 tablespoon lemon juice

1 teaspoon prepared horseradish

6 ounces smoked salmon, flaked

salt and pepper to taste

Mix the first six ingredients until combined. Gently fold in the salmon, salt and pepper. Refrigerate the mixture for a couple of hours and serve as a spread for bagel chips, bread or toast. So good!

SALSA

1 pound fresh tomatoes

2 garlic cloves

2 jalapeño peppers

1/2 cup chopped fresh cilantro or parsley

3 tablespoons chopped fresh peppermint

1/2 teaspoon salt

1 tablespoon lemon juice

Chop the first 3 ingredients together. You can make the pieces as small or large as you like, depending on how chunky you want your salsa. You may also remove the seeds and membranes from the jalapeños if you want to turn down the heat a bit. Place the tomato mixture in a bowl, add the rest of the ingredients, and mix well. Place the salsa in a serving bowl on a platter and surround it with tortilla chips for dipping.

LEMON-TUNA BITES

1 cup albacore tuna (I use canned, but if you use fresh, just broil the tuna steak and flake)
1/4 cup celery, diced
1/4 cup carrots, diced
2 tablespoons finely diced lemon verbena or lemon balm
1/2 to 2/3 cup of mayonnaise

Mix the first 4 ingredients together. Add enough mayonnaise for the mixture to reach a nice spreading consistency. Pile generous spoonsful of the tuna mixture onto bite-sized crackers and arrange on a serving tray.

BASIL WRAPS

One variety of basil is called mammoth. The leaves can grow as big as your hand and are perfect for wraps.

Wash and dry the leaves, place a tablespoon or more of chicken, tuna, or shrimp salad in the middle of each leaf and gently wrap the leaf around the stuffing, tucking in the ends. Use a toothpick to hold the wrap together. Try not to handle the basil too much as it will darken if bruised.

ALCOHOLIC BEVERAGES

Once you've decided what you'll be serving in the food category, it's time to turn your attention to beverages. Here are a few suggestions to get your party off to a good start.

MINT JULEP

4 sprigs of fresh mint
2 1/2 ounces bourbon
1 teaspoon powdered sugar
1 teaspoon water

Place the mint, powdered sugar, and water in the bottom of a glass. Using a wooden spoon, crush the leaves with the sugar and water. Fill the glass with crushed ice and add the bourbon. Stir the mixture and add more ice. Garnish with a mint leaf or two.

Mint julep

MOHITO COCKTAIL

1 teaspoon powdered sugar
juice from 1 lime
4 mint leaves
1 sprig of mint
2 ounces white rum
2 ounces club soda

Place the mint leaves in the bottom of a tall glass and squeeze lime juice over them. Add the powdered sugar and gently crush the mint into the sugar and juice using a long wooden spoon. Fill the glass with crushed ice, add the rum, and stir. Top off with club soda and garnish with a sprig of mint.

ROSE GERANIUM MARTINI

1 cup sugar
1 cup water
2 strips orange zest
1 handful of rose-scented geranium leaves
1/2 cup vodka
1/4 cup Grand Marnier
juice of half an orange
rose geranium blossoms or rose petals

Combine the sugar, water and orange zest in a saucepan over medium heat. Simmer for 2 minutes until the sugar is dissolved. Don't boil or the sugar will darken. Put the geranium leaves in a jar and pour the sugar syrup over them. Seal the jar and let the mixture steep for 2 hours, then drain. Discard the leaves and the zest.

Geranium

Fill a martini shaker with ice and add the vodka, Grand Marnier, orange juice, and 4 tablespoons of the geranium syrup. Shake well and pour into 2 martini glasses. Float a geranium blossom or rose petal in each drink.

LOVING CUP
2 lemons
8 sprigs of lemon balm
1/2 cup sugar
1 bottle champagne
3 1/2 cups water
1/2 bottle Marsala wine
1/2 cup brandy

Lemon balm

Zest 1 lemon and peel the second. Slice both lemons very thin. Put the zest, sliced lemons, lemon balm, and sugar in a large pitcher or jug. Stir in the water, Marsala, and brandy. Cover and chill for 2 hours. Just before serving, strain the chilled mixture and pour into a punch bowl. Add the chilled champagne. Serve in punch cups or wine glasses.

There are also some very pleasant, non-alcoholic drinks made from or enhanced by herbs. Herbal teas are the most common, of course, although there's nothing common about their delectable taste. You can find commercially produced herbal teas in your supermarket, but don't limit yourself to what is on the shelves there.

Specialty shops will have a more adventurous selection. Some of my favorite teas come from the Olive Forge Herb Farm in Haddock, Georgia. They have a wide variety of single flavor teas, ranging from chamomile to lemon verbena to mint. Even better, they've come up with a number of really good combinations. I especially love their orange cinnamon, but all of them are good.

HERBAL TEA

Making your own tea using fresh or dried herbs is easy. You can use any herbs you like, but the most popular are chamomile, mint, lemon verbena, lemon balm, sage, scented geranium, and thyme.

Use either 6 tablespoons of fresh herbs or 3 tablespoons of dried herbs. Place in a teapot, pour 24 ounces of boiling water over them and let the tea steep 3 to 5 minutes. Pour it through a strainer into cups and serve with honey to sweeten.

SPICY GERANIUM TEA

It's simple to perk up any regular tea with herbs.

Place a tea bag in a cup and pour 8 ounces of boiling water over it. Add 3 whole cloves and 2 to 4 rose geranium leaves. Let this steep for 5 minutes. Remove the bag, cloves, and leaves; then sweeten and enjoy. This mixture also makes a refreshing iced tea.

A selection of teas from Olive Forge Herb Farm. Top row, left to right: Lemon Ginger, Chai, Warming Berry. Bottom row: Rooibos Red Bush, Cinnamon Orange, Red Raspberry

Spicy geranium tea

Peppermint water

LEMON BALM TEA
3 parts lemon balm
1 part tarragon
1 part thyme

Use either fresh or dried herbs for this tea. For a 24-ounce pot use 6 tablespoons fresh or 3 tablespoons dried herbs. For a single cup, use a tablespoon of fresh or a teaspoon of dried herbs. Pour boiling water over the herbs, steep for 5 minutes, strain, and serve. This is a nice, relaxing tea and will help soothe a sore throat.

LEMON VERBENA CORDIAL
10 lemon verbena leaves, finely chopped, plus a few leaves for garnish
Juice of 1 lemon
1/4 cup lime juice
1 ounce sugar
2 cups water

Heat all the ingredients in a saucepan, stirring constantly until the sugar is dissolved. Chill in the refrigerator for several hours. Strain and serve over crushed ice in tall glasses. Garnish with lemon verbena leaves.

HERBAL WATER
This sounds very simple, I know, but it's quite refreshing.

Wash two handfuls of spearmint, peppermint, lemon verbena, or bee balm. Lightly bruise the herbs, place them in a pitcher and fill with water. Chill for several hours and serve over ice.

Using a glass pitcher makes an attractive presentation on the table. I keep a pitcher of lemon verbena or peppermint water in the refrigerator all summer.

ENTRÉES

Dinner parties are wonderful opportunities to get a congenial group of people together for a delicious meal, but hosting requires a lot of work. Whenever I can, I like to plan simple main dishes that allow me to enjoy my guests and the food without being exhausted by the preparation. Here are some dishes that impress but don't take hours to prepare.

SALMON EN PAPILLOTE

4 salmon filets
2 lemons
16 sprigs of fresh herbs (marjoram, thyme, oregano, or dill)
olive oil

Place a cookie sheet on the center rack of your oven and pre-heat the oven to 475 degrees. Lay 4 squares of parchment paper on the counter. Place a filet in the center of each square. Squeeze the juice of half a lemon over each filet and lay 4 sprigs of herbs on top of each one. Fold the parchment into packets for the salmon filets, leaving a little room for steam. Then wrap each packet in aluminum foil.

When the oven is ready, place the packets on the hot cookie sheet. Cook for 8 to 10 minutes. Remove the cookie sheet from the oven and carefully open the packets. (Watch out for the steam!) Salt and pepper each filet, drizzle with olive oil and re-cover. Let them sit for 5 minutes before serving.

For a nice effect, you can serve the salmon in the parchment packets (remove the aluminum foil first) and let the diners cut open their own packets. Direct them to salt and pepper the filets and pass lemon slices and a small container of olive oil for drizzling. Serves four.

TARRAGON-STUFFED CHICKEN BREASTS

4 boneless, skinless chicken breasts
4 tablespoons softened butter
2 tablespoons chopped tarragon
salt and pepper to taste

Preheat the oven to 375 degrees. Combine the tarragon and butter. Cut a slit in the side of each chicken breast. Put one-fourth of the herbed butter inside each breast. Salt and pepper the chicken.

    Place the breasts in a lightly greased baking dish, cover with aluminum foil, and bake for 30 minutes. Remove the foil and bake for another 10 minutes to brown the breasts. Serves four.

SHRIMP AND HERB PASTA FOR TWO

6 ounces of pasta (any kind you like)
12–16 large shrimp, peeled and deveined
2 cloves garlic, each cut in four pieces
1/2 cup fresh basil leaves
1 teaspoon fresh ginger, grated
2 tablespoons broken pecan pieces
2 tablespoons butter
1 tablespoon lime juice
salt and pepper to taste

While cooking the pasta according to package directions, melt the butter in a medium skillet. Sauté the garlic pieces in the butter for a couple of minutes, then remove and discard. Sauté the shrimp in the butter until opaque; stir in the ginger. Remove the skillet from the heat. When the pasta is done, add it to the shrimp in the skillet. Add the pecans, basil and lime juice. Toss and serve.

Shrimp and herb pasta

BEEF AND HERB STUFFED SHELLS

1 package jumbo pasta shells
2 pounds lean ground beef
2 eggs, beaten
1/4 cup grated Parmesan cheese
1/3 cup breadcrumbs
1 tablespoon each chopped fresh oregano, basil, and parsley
  (1 teaspoon, if dried)
salt and pepper to taste
16 ounces shredded mozzarella cheese
1 large jar of marinara sauce

Preheat the oven to 350 degrees. Cook the shells as directed on the package and set aside to drain. Brown the beef in a non-stick skillet and drain off the fat. In a large mixing bowl, combine the beef, eggs, Parmesan, breadcrumbs, herbs, salt, and pepper.

Spread a couple of large spoonsful of the sauce in the bottom of one very large or two medium baking dishes. Stuff the shells with the meat mixture. Arrange the stuffed shells in the dishes. Pour the rest of the sauce over the shells and bake for 20 minutes. Remove from the oven and sprinkle the shells with a good layer of the mozzarella cheese. Return them to the oven for 10 minutes until the cheese is well melted. Kids especially love this dish. Serves four.

TOMATO PIE

1 9-inch pre-baked deep-dish pie shell
5 tomatoes, peeled and sliced
10–15 large fresh basil leaves
1 bunch green onions, chopped
1 cup shredded mozzarella cheese
1 cup shredded cheddar cheese
1 cup mayonnaise
salt and pepper

Preheat the oven to 350 degrees. Peel and slice the tomatoes. Spread a clean dishtowel in the bottom of the sink and lay the tomatoes on it. Sprinkle them with salt and let them sit for 10 to 15 minutes to drain. Then alternately layer the tomatoes, basil and green onion in the pie shell. Season with salt and pepper. Mix the two cheeses together. Gently fold the mayonnaise into the cheeses. Spread the cheese mixture over the tomatoes. Place a thin collar of aluminum foil around the edge of the pastry to keep it from burning. Bake for 30 minutes or until lightly browned. Let the pie cool for about 15 minutes before cutting and serving. Serves six to eight.

Basil

STEAK WITH BASIL AND GARLIC

2 New York strip steaks
4 cloves garlic
3 tablespoons butter
1 handful basil leaves
salt and pepper

Salt and pepper the steaks and let them stand at room temperature for about half an hour. When you're ready to cook, melt the butter in a medium skillet. Add the garlic and sauté for a minute or two, then remove and discard. Add the basil and stir until the leaves are wilted. Increase the heat slightly and place the steaks in the pan. Cook for 4 to 5 minutes on each side or to your desired level of doneness. Remove the steaks to waiting plates, leaving the basil leaves in the skillet. Let sit for 3 or 4 minutes to settle the juices, then serve. Serves two.

SAVORY HAMBURGERS

1 pound lean ground beef
3 tablespoons of chopped fresh herbs (any mixture you like of thyme, basil, marjoram, and oregano)
1 teaspoon soy sauce
1 egg, beaten
1/8 to 1/4 cup bread crumbs
salt and pepper to taste

Mix the ground beef with next 3 ingredients. Add enough breadcrumbs to keep the mixture together and workable. Shape into four patties and salt and pepper them. Cook as you do any hamburger. Serve on toasted buns with your choice of condiments.

Chicken roulades

CHICKEN ROULADES

4 boneless, skinless chicken breasts
1 cup flat parsley leaves
1/4 cup oregano leaves
2/3 cup shredded mozzarella cheese
1 egg, beaten
breadcrumbs

Preheat the oven to 350 degrees. Pound each breast between two sheets of waxed paper until very thin. Salt and pepper the breasts. Chop the herbs and spread one-fourth of the mixture on each breast. Then spread evenly with the cheese. Carefully roll up the breasts into logs and tuck in the ends. Secure each log with one or two toothpicks.

Beat the egg. Dip each breast into the egg and then roll in the bread-crumbs to cover. Place the breasts in a baking dish that has been lightly oiled and bake for 25 to 30 minutes. Remove the toothpicks and serve on yellow rice. Serves four.

SIDES

Every great entrée deserves a side dish that is worthy of it. Here are a few of my favorites.

HERBED POTATOES

4 cups red potatoes, cut into 1-inch cubes
olive oil
1 tablespoon chopped rosemary
2 tablespoons chopped marjoram
salt

Preheat the oven to 375 degrees. Place the potatoes in a large bowl, drizzle with olive oil, and sprinkle with the herbs. Toss and arrange the potatoes in a single layer in a baking dish or on a cookie sheet.

Bake for 30 minutes, stirring once after 15 minutes. When done, remove from the oven, salt to taste, and stir once more before serving. Serves four to six.

BROILED TOMATOES

2 large tomatoes, washed and cut in half
1 tablespoon grated Parmesan cheese
4 teaspoons breadcrumbs
2 teaspoons chopped fresh oregano
4 teaspoons butter
salt and pepper

Preheat the oven broiler. Arrange the tomato halves in a small baking dish. Salt and pepper the tomatoes. Mix the cheese, breadcrumbs, and oregano and sprinkle the top of each tomato with the mixture. Top each tomato slice with a teaspoon of butter.

Pour enough water into the dish to cover the bottom. Place the pan under the broiler for 10 to 15 minutes until the topping is browned. Serves four.

GRILLED ASPARAGUS

25–30 fresh asparagus spears
olive oil
1 tablespoon lemon thyme, chopped
salt

Preheat the oven to 350 degrees. Wash the asparagus and remove the tough lower stalks. Peel the remaining stalks if necessary. Arrange the asparagus in a single layer in a baking dish. Drizzle with olive oil, sprinkle with salt and the chopped lemon thyme. Bake for 15 to 20 minutes. Serves four to six.

RICE WITH HERBS

1 cup long grain rice
2 tablespoons butter
2 cups chicken stock
1/2 teaspoon chopped fresh basil
1 teaspoon chopped fresh thyme
1 teaspoon minced fresh rosemary

Preheat the oven to 350 degrees. Bring the stock to a boil in a saucepan. Melt the butter in a medium skillet. Sauté the rice a minute or two in the butter. Then add the stock and herbs to the skillet and bring to a simmer. Transfer the mixture to a casserole dish, cover and bake for 45 minutes. Serves four to six.

Soups and salads can sparkle with herbal flavor whether they accompany a meal or are served alone.

POTATO SOUP

4 cups potatoes, peeled and chopped
3 cups onions, chopped
1 bouquet garni
1 1/2 to 2 quarts water (enough to cover potatoes and onions in the
   pan)
2 1/2 tablespoons powdered chicken stock
2 to 3 tablespoons butter
1/2 pint cream
salt and pepper to taste
1 tablespoon fresh chives, chopped

In a large saucepan, bring the first 6 ingredients to a boil. Reduce the heat and simmer for 45 minutes or until the potatoes and onions are soft. Remove from the heat and remove and discard the herbs. In 4 or 5 batches, put the mixture into blender, blend until smooth and return to the pan. Add butter, cream, salt, and pepper. Reheat and serve. Garnish with the chives. Serves six to eight.

CARROT AND LEMON THYME SOUP

2 1/2 cups sliced carrots
1 onion, diced
1 potato, diced
1 apple, diced
1 cup chicken broth
1/4 cup finely diced lemon thyme
1–2 cups water
1 tablespoon orange juice
1/2 cup cream
lemon thyme leaves for garnish
sour cream

Place the first 6 ingredients in a saucepan and add enough water just to cover. Bring the mixture to a boil. Simmer for about 45 minutes, until all the pieces are very soft. Remove from the heat and let cool for 30 minutes.

   Puree the soup in a blender or food processor, in several batches if necessary, until smooth. Return it to the pan and add the cream and orange juice. Reheat and serve. Garnish with the lemon thyme leaves and swirl a teaspoonful of sour cream on the top. Serves four to six.

Thyme

Carrot and lemon thyme soup

FLORAL GARDEN SALAD
3 cups salad greens
2 tablespoons chopped pecans
1/3 cup golden raisins
Herbal vinaigrette dressing**
1/2 cup **edible flowers***

Toss the first 3 ingredients with enough dressing to cover. Sprinkle the flowers across the top of the salad and garnish with two goat cheese medallions. Serves four.

*EDIBLE FLOWERS
There are many edible flowers, but these are probably the most common and easiest to find: flowers of all culinary herbs, dandelion petals, honeysuckle, nasturtium, pansy, rose petals, squash blossoms, violets

**HERBAL VINAIGRETTE DRESSING
3 tablespoons olive oil
1 tablespoon red wine vinegar (or an herbal vinegar of your choice)
1/4 teaspoon dried mustard
1 crushed and peeled garlic clove
3 tablespoons fresh, chopped herbs (basil, chives, or lemon balm are
   good, but use what you like)
salt and pepper

Add all the ingredients to a medium-sized bottle and shake well.

GOAT CHEESE MEDALLIONS

1 8-ounce package of creamy goat cheese, softened

1 tablespoon maple syrup (real maple syrup, not "maple-flavored" pancake syrup)

1 teaspoon fresh lemon verbena or pineapple sage leaves, finely chopped

1/3 to 1/2 cup chopped pecans

Mix the first 3 ingredients well in a small bowl. Refrigerate half an hour to make handling easier. Shape the cheese mixture in 1 1/2 inch balls. Flatten slightly and press the medallions into the pecans to coat. Keep refrigerated until time to serve.

Pineapple sage

Garden salad with rosemary flowers and goat cheese medallion

These are tasty additions to any salad. Place one or two on the side of the plate to be eaten along with the greens.

PASTA AND SHRIMP SALAD
8 ounces small shell pasta
2 pounds cooked, peeled, and deveined shrimp
1 medium tomato, peeled, seeded and chopped
1 cucumber, peeled and chopped
1/2 cup shredded carrots
1 tablespoon fresh sage, chopped
1 tablespoon fresh parsley, chopped
salt and pepper to taste

Dressing:
1/2 cup plain yogurt
1/2 cup bottled Italian dressing
salt and pepper

Cook the pasta as directed on the package and drain. Combine the pasta with the shrimp, tomato, cucumber, carrots, sage, and parsley. Add salt and pepper to taste. To make the dressing, whisk together the last three ingredients. Toss the salad ingredients with the dressing and serve.

Note: Don't add the dressing until you're ready to serve because the pasta will absorb it and become mushy. Serves four.

TARRAGON CUCUMBER SALAD

8 cucumbers, peeled and sliced into rounds
2 sweet onions, like Vidalias, chopped
1 cup plain yogurt
1/4 cup herbal tarragon vinegar
1 teaspoon salt
fresh ground pepper to taste
1 tablespoon finely chopped tarragon
1 tablespoon shelled sunflower seeds

Combine the cucumbers and onions in a mixing bowl. In a smaller bowl, mix the next 5 ingredients well with a whisk. Pour the dressing over the vegetables, toss and refrigerate 3 to 4 hours before serving. Pass sunflower seeds as a topping.

Sunflower seeds

DESSERTS

Finish your meal with one of these easy, herby treats.

ROSE GERANIUM RICE PUDDING

1 cup long grain rice
2 cups milk
8 rose scented geranium leaves
1 ounce flaked coconut
2 cups chopped almonds or pecans
2 ounces raisins
1/4 cup light brown sugar
whipping cream
1 tablespoon sugar

Preheat the oven to 375 degrees. Mix the rice and milk in a saucepan and add 4 geranium leaves. Cover and simmer for 30 minutes. Remove from the heat. Discard the leaves. Add the coconut, almonds, raisins, and brown sugar. Stir well and turn into a buttered baking dish. Place the remaining leaves on the top of the pudding and bake for 45 minutes. Whip the cream with a tablespoon of sugar until soft peaks form. Serve the pudding in dessert dishes and top with the whipped cream. Serves four to six.

SUMMER FRUIT COMPOTE

1 cup **simple syrup**＊
6 sprigs opal or purple basil
1 cup lemon verbena leaves
4 sprigs mint
2 cups cubed cantaloupe
2 cups cubed honeydew melon
2 cups peaches, peeled, cubed, and sprinkled with lemon juice
whipping cream

*Combine the syrup with the herbs and refrigerate for 24 hours. Remove
the herbs from the syrup and discard. Gently mix the fruit and syrup.
Whip the cream with sugar to taste. Spoon the fruit mixture into dessert
bowls and top each one with a dollop of whipped cream. Serves eight.*

＊SIMPLE SYRUP

*Put 1/2 cup of sugar and 1/2 cup of water in a saucepan. Heat until sugar
completely dissolves. That's all there is to it.*

LAVENDER COOKIES

2 eggs
1 stick butter
1 cup sugar
1 teaspoon lavender leaves, finely chopped
1 1/2 cups flour
2 teaspoons baking powder
1/2 teaspoon salt
lavender water＊
powdered sugar

Preheat the oven to 375 degrees. Cream the eggs, butter, and sugar with a mixer on low. Add the lavender and mix an additional minute or two. Sift the dry ingredients into a medium bowl. Add the butter mixture and stir until well blended. Using a teaspoon, drop the dough onto an ungreased cookie sheet. Bake 8 to 10 minutes or until lightly browned. Cool the cookies on a rack.

Make the frosting by mixing enough lavender water and sugar to make a smooth, spreadable frosting. Add a drop of red and a couple of drops of blue food coloring, if desired, for lavender-tinted frosting. Ice the cookies and let them sit uncovered until the frosting has set.

*LAVENDER WATER
2 cups of water
Generous handful of washed and bruised lavender leaves

Combine the two ingredients in a jar. Bruise the leaves with a wooden spoon. Seal and refrigerate for 2 days. Strain the liquid and store it in the refrigerator in a sealed bottle or jar.

GLAZED BANANAS OVER ICE CREAM
3 firm bananas, peeled, cut lengthwise, then cut in thirds
2 tablespoons butter
1/4 cup light brown sugar
1/4 cup orange juice
1 teaspoon fresh, finely chopped pineapple sage leaves

Heat the butter, brown sugar, juice, and pineapple sage in a medium skillet until bubbly. Sauté the banana pieces in the pan, turning frequently, for 5 minutes. Serve immediately over vanilla ice cream.

Lavender cookies

CHAPTER 4

Crafts

NE OF THE THINGS I MOST ENJOY is making gifts for the people I
love. Unfortunately the gifts haven't always been popular. My
friends and relatives have endured a lot over the years. Although
I tried hard, I never advanced beyond some bumpy-looking scarves
and shawls when I took up crocheting. Baking wasn't my strongest
talent either. I'm never sure when cookies are really done, so I've given
away hundreds of over-baked, rock-hard sugar cookies. They might
have been nicely decorated, but all the icing in the world couldn't
really save them.

I think we were all relieved when I started making herbal gifts.
Food products are what most people would expect from an herb
grower, and I've certainly handed out my share of those. Herbal vine-
gars and flavored honeys are always favorites.

Herbal teas are also popular. One year I made my own teas and
spent the weeks before Christmas scouring flea markets and antique
malls until I finally found enough old china teapots to give one to
everybody on my list along with a packet of tea.

Not all herbal gifts have to be culinary. Here are some other
suggestions.

Wreaths

Wreaths are attractive decorations with the added bonus of fragrance. They can be as simple or as elaborate as you like. Use dried or fresh herbs. If you're using dried herbs, a week or two before assembling your wreath, tie small bundles of herbs together to dry. If you're going to use fresh herbs, just cut and tie them into bundles when you're ready to assemble the wreath.

Wreath forms come in several varieties. At your local craft store, you'll find forms made of grapevines, straw, wire, Styrofoam, and plastic. Once you've chosen your form and your herb bundles are ready, it's time to make your wreath.

Working so that your bundles all face the same direction, begin fastening the herbs to the wreath using florist wire or fern pins. With the grapevine forms, you can often just wedge the herbs between the stems of the vines. Be sure to overlap the bundles so that you'll get a fuller effect and cover the tied stems. In addition to the herbs, dried flowers can be added to the wreath for more color. Once your wreath is complete, fashion a hanger on the back with more of the florist wire, and your creation will be ready to hang.

Any herbs can be used for wreath making. The choice often depends on which ones you have on hand and the look you're after. Some of my favorites for wreaths, not only for appearance but also for their fragrance, are lavender, rosemary, sweet Annie, curry plant, marjoram, and thyme.

Bookmarks

In Victorian times when young ladies wanted to preserve a floral souvenir, they pressed the flowers between the pages of large books to dry. Today you can dry flowers or leaves in the same old-fashioned way—laying them carefully between sheets of waxed paper and placing them between the pages of a thick book—or you can use a

calibracoa hybrid

"Million Bells"

flower press, which you can find at a hobby or craft shop. However you do it, you should check your flowers for dryness after a couple of weeks.

Of course, once they're dry, flowers and sprigs of herbs are just dried flowers and leaves. What do you do with them? One thing you might want to try is making bookmarks. They're simple to construct and quite lovely. All you need is a laminating machine and a little time. Just about every office supply store has a laminating machine and will only charge you a nominal amount for using it.

Following the directions at the store, simply lay your dried herbs and flowers between two lamination sheets, being careful to leave enough room between the herbs for cutting. Laminate and then cut the sheet into bookmark-sized pieces. You can make them rectangular for a traditional look or cut around the actual shape of the flower or plant for something a little different. Whichever design you choose, you'll end up with colorful, delicate-looking bookmarks that you'll be proud to give away (maybe with a copy of this book).

While the old ways are still good, that doesn't mean technology has no part to play in herbal crafts. In fact, I couldn't do without it.

One lazy summer afternoon in 2002 when I had nothing else to do, I put a couple of fresh flowers into my computer scanner and pushed the button. I had no plan, just wanted to see what would happen. The result was dramatic—a beautiful, nearly three-dimensional image of the flowers.

Once I saw the printed product, I had to find something to do with it. Here are a couple of projects I came up with.

Framed Botanicals

This was an obvious use of the scanned images. Printed on card or parchment stock, they became exquisite, full-color botanicals, similar to the plates found in old books. Using a nice handwriting font, the scientific and common names of a flower or herb can be printed right on the picture. In a pretty frame, it looks like something that has been professionally produced.

Notecards

The same scanned images can be used as note cards, employing simple word processing. Just position two of the images on the right side of a standard letter-size page. Print, cut and fold. The cards will fit in a standard invitation envelope.

Place Mats

Back in the early 2000s, we lived in Macon, Georgia, and I fell in love with the city, our house, and our yard where everything seemed to flourish. I knew our time there would end in a few years, and I wanted to remember every flower and every leaf. I used my scanner, made copies of plants and blossoms in every season and created place mats.

I scanned and printed hundreds of images, then cut out each one so that there was no background, only the leaf or flower. Then I glued them onto corkboards and painted over them with several coats of decoupage glue. Now when I see at them on my table, I'm reminded of the beauty of my former home.

Chives

Bay

Basil

CHAPTER 5

The Most Common Herbs for Growing

THE FOLLOWING PAGES aren't meant to be a complete herbal index. Instead, they're my short list of the most commonly used and grown herbs.

Basil

Basil is a perennial native to India, but it was cultivated in Europe as early as the sixteenth century. And we've embraced it with gusto in this country where it grows as an annual. A culinary favorite, it is the primary ingredient in pesto and is used in salads and main dishes alike. It's hard to imagine homegrown tomatoes without basil. There are a number of varieties of basil—sweet, lemon, Thai, mammoth, globe, and opal, to name a few.

Bay

Everywhere except in the very deep South, this tender evergreen, also known as sweet bay and bay laurel, is best grown in containers that can be brought inside over the winter. Use a bay leaf or two in stews, soups and sauces (just remember to remove the leaves before serving). It's also one of the ingredients in bouquet garni.

Chives

Chives are a perennial member of the onion family and are used in cooking all over the world. Easy to grow in the smallest garden spot, chives can be used in salads, sauces, and as a garnish for vegetable dishes. The flowers are often tossed in salads and the minced greens add color and additional flavor to mashed potatoes and potato salad.

Cilantro

People either love or hate this annual herb. A mainstay of Latin cooking, cilantro can be used in everything from vegetables and meat dishes to desserts. It looks a lot like flat-leaf parsley, but one small sniff will clear up any confusion.

Dill

One of the biblical herbs, dill can perk up the flavor of soups, fish, and breads. Everyone knows dill flavors pickles, but did you know it also can be added to cakes and apple pie as well? This annual herb looks very much like fennel, but the tastes and fragrances are quite different.

Fennel

This feathery perennial can grow to a height of several feet, so take that into consideration when planting it. The delicate, licorice-like flavor of the leaves is a nice addition to salads, soups, and vegetable dishes. The Florence variety produces a large bulb that can be sliced raw into salads or cooked as a root vegetable.

Lavender

One whiff of this perennial herb will transport you to an earlier, more romantic time. Although lavender has its culinary uses—most notably as an ingredient in the classic herbes de Provence mixture—it is most often employed in soaps, perfumes, lotions, and potpourris.

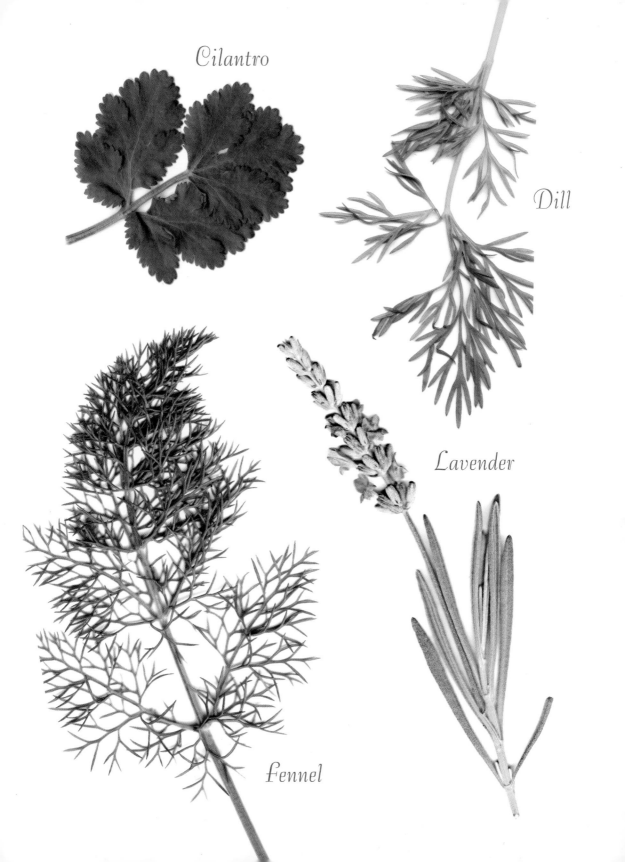

Cilantro

Dill

Lavender

Fennel

Lemon Verbena

Lemon Balm

Mint

Marjoram

Lemon Balm

Perennial lemon balm is also called melissa and some folks in the Middle Ages believed it could revive a dying person. We now know it doesn't have lifesaving properties, but it makes delightful teas—on its own or added to black or green tea—and is used in jams, wine cups, and salads.

Lemon Verbena

Lemon verbena is a perennial in most parts of the South, especially if it's cut back and heavily mulched in early winter. Its sharp, lemony scent makes this a fine herb for teas, fruit salads, cakes and other desserts. It's also a favorite ingredient for long-lasting potpourris and sachets.

Marjoram

Once planted, this Mediterranean perennial comes back to your garden year after year. It's a sweet, spicy herb that can be added to sauces, meat dishes, and salads, or infused as a tea. Its distinct aroma is a pleasant addition to potpourris.

Mints

There are more than 600 varieties of this hardy perennial in the world. In addition to the commonplace peppermint, spearmint, and catnip, you can also find chocolate mint, apple mint, and even eau de cologne mint. Use mint in teas, syrups, salads, and drinks. Just be careful where you plant it. It's very, very invasive.

Oregano

Oregano is a perennial herb that is at the heart of Italian cooking. It's a staple in pizza, pasta dishes, and salads. Added to a dry rub, oregano gives roasted meat a bright, piquant flavor. There are several varieties, including a spicy oregano, that will bring a bit of heat to your dishes.

Parsley

Parsley is a biennial, which means it lives only two years. Just about any recipe can benefit from parsley because it has the unique ability to intensify the other flavors in a dish. Use it in salads, vegetables, soups, stews, and sauces. You can also chew a leaf or two to freshen your breath.

Rosemary

Rosemary is a dependable evergreen shrub. Recent studies have proved that just smelling rosemary gives the memory a boost. It also shines in meat dishes, especially lamb and pork. To infuse grilled food with extra flavor, strip the leaves from rosemary branches and use them as skewers for meat or vegetables.

Sage

A hardy perennial, sage is a favorite ingredient in meat dishes. What Thanksgiving feast is complete without sage dressing? Medicinally, it's said to aid digestion and, in tea form, soothe coughing.

Oregano

Sage

Rosemary

Parsley

Tarragon

Thyme

Scented
Geranium

Scented Geranium

This marvelous herb is an African native but is now grown all over the world by people who love its intoxicating fragrance. There are several varieties, including citrus, oak leaf, mint, and apple, but the favorite is probably the rose. Widely used in cosmetics and aromatics, scented geranium is also good in salads, desserts, drinks, and jellies.

Tarragon

The classic French tarragon doesn't thrive in our hot, moist Southern summers and cold winters. It can be grown here if you find a sheltered spot for it where it doesn't get too much afternoon sun and where it is protected from winter winds. A good alternative is Mexican (or Texas) tarragon. Its flavor is more robust than the French variety, but it is a hardy perennial here. Use tarragon in salads, cheese dishes, soups, vegetables, and pastas.

Thyme

Thyme, a low-growing perennial, is often an evergreen in the South. It comes in numerous varieties—common, English, silver, lemon, and golden, among others. The tiny leaves are often used in sauces, stuffings, and soups. Thyme complements meat and vegetable dishes alike and is said to aid in the digestion of fats. As a tea, it soothes sore throats and eases coughing.

Essential oils

CHAPTER 6

Aromatherapy

NO BOOK ON HERBS WOULD BE COMPLETE without including a mention of aromatherapy. Aromatherapy is the use of scents (either from the plants themselves or from essential oils made from herbs, spices, trees, and flowers) to benefit the mind and body. Making essential oils is a complex and expensive process that is best left to professional laboratories, but the oils themselves are readily obtainable in herb shops, nutritional shops, and online.

Here are some of the most popular fragrances and their properties.

Uplifting	Energizing	Refreshing	Relaxing
Basil	Citrus	Chamomile	Marjoram
Bergamot	Peppermint	Cypress	Chamomile
Lemon Balm	Rose	Geranium	Lavender
Sage	Orange	Rosemary	Pine
Jasmine	Rosemary	Rose Geranium	Vanilla

Herbal fragrances are simple to use. I prefer the oils because their fragrances are stronger and longer lasting. To surround yourself with scent, put a few drops of essential oil on a tissue or handkerchief and tuck it into your pocket or waistband. Ten drops of your favorite oil in a warm bath will fill the room with fragrance. If you take showers instead, put a few drops of the essential oil on your washcloth or loofah. A quick cure for insomnia is placing a drop of lavender, sage, or chamomile oil on the underside of your pillow.

Essential oils can be used as room fresheners, either as sprays or potpourris:

Air Freshening Spray

Fill an atomizer with a pint of isopropyl alcohol. Add 100 drops of essential oil in a combination of your choice. Fill up the bottle with distilled or bottled water and shake well. Use it like any other air freshener.

Easy Room Freshener

Place a small bowl of warm water on a sunny windowsill. Add a few drops of the essential oil of your choice. The warmth will dispense the fragrance into the air.

CITRUS POTPOURRI

2 cups dried lemon verbena leaves
1 cup dried spearmint leaves
1 cup dried lemon thyme leaves
1/2 cup dried peppermint leaves
1/2 cup dried bee balm leaves
1/2 cup dried lemon balm leaves
2/3 cup dried lemon peel
3 drops lemon essential oil
3 drops orange essential oil

Combine all the ingredients except the oil in a large bowl. Mix gently with your hands, taking care not to crumble the herbs. Add the essential oils one drop at a time, mixing the leaves after each drop. Put the mixture in a container and seal. Store in a dark, cool place for six to eight weeks. After it's seasoned, place the mixture in attractive bowls to display it. The scent will last longer if you have lids for the bowls and only remove them when you want to enjoy the aroma.

QUICK POTPOURRI

If you don't have the time to let traditional potpourri season, this is a quick substitute. Put 1/4 cup clay cat litter (the plain, unscented, cheap variety) into a small pottery dish or bowl. Add 30–40 drops of essential oil and mix well. If you like, add a teaspoon or two of dried herbs or fresh herb flowers for color.

CHAPTER 7

Bath and Beauty

FROM ANCIENT TIMES, herbs have been part of beauty regimens. Egyptian women used herb-scented oils to soften their skin as early as 10,000 BC. In ancient Greece marjoram, thyme, rose, and sage were infused in olive oil to make expensive ointments for skin care and perfumes. Roman women mixed burnt almonds, charred rose petals, and antimony to make eyeliner. Herbs are used extensively in today's beauty products. Here are some modern beauty and bath recipes you can make for yourself.

SCENTED BATH CRYSTALS
1 cup coarse kosher salt
20–30 drops essential oil
food coloring, if desired

Combine the salt and essential oil in a small bowl. Keep mixing until there is no trace of liquid. If you choose to tint the bath salt, add 2 or 3 drops of food coloring at a time, mixing to disperse the liquid and until you achieve the color you want. Put it into a pretty container. Add a tablespoon or two to a warm bath and enjoy.

HERBAL BATH BAGS

Tie a handful of fresh herbs (lavender, lemon verbena, mint, or rosemary) into a square of cheesecloth. Gather the ends and tie them with twine to make a bag. Leave the ends of the twine long enough to attach the bag to the faucet in your bathtub. Position the bag so that the water runs through it when you're filling the tub. It will scent the water and the steam rising off of it.

CLEANSING FACIAL STEAM

Place two handfuls of fresh herbs—either lavender, sage, rosemary, or mint—in a large bowl and pour very hot water over them. Pull back your hair. Tent a large bath towel over your head and the bowl. Steam your face for 5 minutes, then wash with a gentle cleanser and moisturize.

GENTLE FACIAL MASK—This is a calming mask that will soothe and gently soften your skin.

In a blender, mix 2 handfuls of fresh herbs (mint, thyme, or lavender) and 2 tablespoons of bottled or distilled water. Blend at high speed for 5 seconds. Pour into a bowl and add 1–3 teaspoons of oatmeal to the mixture to get to spreading texture. Spread on your face and leave for 20 minutes. Remove with warm water.

CHAPTER 8

Herbal Medicine Cabinet

H ERBS HAVE ALWAYS PLAYED AN IMPORTANT ROLE in healing. Although herbal medicine is often considered alternative treatment today, many plants used over the centuries are now part of mainstream pharmacology. A good example of this is foxglove. Ancient healers used it to treat heart problems; modern physicians prescribe a derivative of the plant, digitalis, to their cardiac patients.

I don't pretend to be an herbalist and would never suggest a remedy for any serious ailment. If you are ill, you should see a doctor. However, I have listed here some simple aids for minor injuries and complaints.

BRUISES AND SPRAINS

Many athletes already know that arnica (a member of the sunflower family that has been used medicinally since the 1500s) helps to reduce the pain and swelling of bruises and sprains. You can find it in oil or cream form in most nutritional stores. It should be used only on unbroken skin. Witch hazel and tea tree oil also sooth bruises.

BURNS

The cool, gelatinous inside of aloe vera leaves will bring immediate relief to the pain of burns and will speed healing. Aloe vera also soothes sunburns. Grow this succulent in a pot on a sunny windowsill, and you'll always have some when you need it.

Colds and Sore Throats

Sage or thyme tea is soothing for a sore throat, particularly if honey and lemon are added, and may temporarily reduce the symptoms of a cold. Make the tea with one tablespoon of fresh or one teaspoon of dried herbs and 8 ounces of boiling water. Strain into a mug and add honey and lemon.

Indigestion

Peppermint tea will relax your intestinal tract and relieve painful gas. It also eases nausea and heartburn.

Insect Bites or Stings

Tea tree oil is a powerhouse of antibacterial and anti-inflammatory properties. Just rub it on the affected area. Witch hazel is also good for bites and stings.

Insomnia

Chamomile tea will relax you and make it easier to drift off to sleep. Lavender, valerian, catnip, and hops are other mildly sedative teas.

Nausea

A piece or two of candied ginger or a cup of tea made with a tablespoon of powdered ginger will stop or ease nausea. Taken before and during a trip, it often prevents motion sickness. Chewing a couple of pieces of candied ginger sometimes stops hiccoughs, too. Another remedy for nausea is peppermint tea.

Tension Headaches

Try valerian tea or an infusion of lavender (1/4 cup lavender leaves or blossoms infused for 5 minutes in 8 ounces of boiling water) to treat tension headaches. A drop of lavender oil on your temples also may help.

Toothache

If the pain is due to a cavity, put a drop or two of oil of cloves on a cotton ball and hold it directly on the tooth. This will temporarily ease the pain until you can get to a dentist.

Candied ginger

Herbal magic has been used for centuries,
long before this medieval Irish tower was built.

CHAPTER 9

Magic, Potions, and Spells

LET ME START WITH AN APOLOGY TO MY READERS who are serious about growing and using herbs and not interested in nonsense. This section is not supposed to be taken seriously, but the subject is so much fun I couldn't resist. Herbs have been ingredients in magic potions and spells as long as humans have searched for ways to control their world. Here are some superstitious uses for herbs that I've run across over the years. I have no reason to believe they do anything other than provide mild amusement.

·⊶⊰⊱⊷·

Basil

Soak dried basil leaves in water for three days, then sprinkle the water at your doorstep to attract money and success. Basil can also be employed to increase the love in your home. To do this, put half a cup of dried basil leaves in an open bowl in your kitchen. You have to change the leaves every week. If you're going to rely on this method for keeping a happy home, you'd better plant a lot of basil.

Bay

Place a few bay leaves in a small bag and tie it with ribbon. Wear the bag around your neck to stop people from interfering with your life. If it were me, I'd just tell them to mind their own business and wear a pretty necklace instead.

Catnip

Here's a potion to attract a new lover: Under a full moon, soak catnip leaves in whiskey for an hour. Then sprinkle the whiskey on your doorstep. Repeat this every day for three weeks. You'll either attract a new lover or a bunch of drunken cats.

Dill

If you've been jinxed or crossed in love, mix dill leaves with salt and scatter the mixture around your house to break the evil spell. It might work, but someone's still going to have to clean up all that salt.

Fennel

Fennel seed and dried oregano carried in a flannel bag in your pocket is said to keep the law away. As a former police officer, I'm not sure I like the sound of this one.

Ginger

The root of this spicy plant, dried, and kept under your pillow, is said to increase passion in your love life. It may, but some of that ardor just might fade if your lover finds a nasty, dried root in your bed.

Lavender

Make a tiny bag, fill it with dried lavender blossoms, and tuck it into your bra. This little sachet is supposed to make you irresistible to members of both sexes. I have to ask—is this something you really want?

Lemon Verbena

If you want to break up a couple and bring about a divorce, this spell is just the ticket. First, steal a piece of clothing from each person. Then put a branch of lemon verbena between the pieces, wrap the whole thing in a piece of cloth, and bury it under the couple's porch. It might work, but you could end up in jail for theft and trespassing, too.

Marjoram

Place some dried marjoram leaves in a corner of every room of your house to ward off bad luck and electrical shocks. I don't know about the bad luck, but if you're really having a problem with electrical shocks, call an electrician. That's dangerous!

Mint

To keep your enemies away, make a tea with mint leaves and wash your floors with it. Maybe I'm being too picky, but wouldn't you just have to immediately rewash the floors to get the tea off?

Oregano

Oregano is supposed to be useful if you're having legal troubles. While you're waiting to go to trial, you should burn dried oregano on charcoal and pray for deliverance. Hiring a good attorney would be another smart move.

Rosemary

To ensure that she's the dominant person in the relationship and that her man will never stray, a woman should plant rosemary by her front door. Rosemary is also effective for keeping away pests. One of those pests might be a flirtatious neighbor who has her sights on your husband.

Sage

Set several branches of dried sage on fire. Hold them in your right hand, wave them around and walk through your house spreading the smoke to cleanse and purify the spirits in your home. Tip: make sure your fire insurance premiums are current.

Thyme

Burn dried thyme on charcoal and breathe in the smoke to stop nightmares. It could be effective, but this just doesn't sound like a healthy activity to me.

A bouquet of mint, fennel, rosemary, bee balm, tarragon, and scented geranium

Index

Facing page: Madison McDonald, Ashley White, and Devyn Cone—the author's granddaughters—climb a Cottonwood. Seed pods from the tree are used in flower arrangements and the wood is used by artisans.